Vox Populi

---

600 Latin Quotes and Phrases for Everyday Life and Personal Inspiration

Giulio Vitali, Richard Lawson

KARMA
STUDIO

KARMA
STUDIO

Table of Contents

VOX POPULI
Latin expression

— Literally "voice of the people," meaning the common sentiment or the opinion of the majority. The phrase is often remembered in its proverbial form "Vox populi, vox Dei" ("the voice of the people is the voice of God"), which attributes to popular will a kind of moral—and almost sacred—authority.

The Mouth of Truth, an ancient Roman symbol of truth and justice.

What's the point of Latin today?

Vox populi. The voice of the people.

Two words carried intact from ancient Rome to our own time. There is no greater force than words shared—words passed from mouth to mouth, surviving trends and centuries, and becoming part of our common heritage.

Latin has this rare power: it can compress a universal idea into just a few syllables and keep it alive for millennia. People often call Latin a "dead" language, but that phrase is already a contradiction. Latin has never truly died—it lives on in our everyday speech, in the mottos we repeat, in the laws that shape our justice system, and in the ideas that built philosophy, science, and religion.

So, what's the point of Latin today?
It sharpens our understanding of English, which draws nearly half of its vocabulary from Latin. And it gives a huge advantage to anyone who wants to study the Romance languages—Spanish, French, Portuguese, and Romanian are its direct descendants. Latin is also essential in fields like medicine, law, music, and theology. But above all, it trains us to think with clarity, because it strips language down to its essence.

This book brings together 600 timeless Latin sayings—quotations, proverbs, and maxims handed down by great orators, thinkers, poets, and men of faith. They still speak to us with surprising relevance. You don't need to be a scholar to enjoy them. These are sparks of wisdom you can use in conversation, to impress a friend, or simply to inspire yourself each day.

The gift of Latin is this: to remind us that a word is never just a word. It is voice, root, and culture. It is what binds us together as a community, then and now.

Vox populi: the people's voice, still speaking across the centuries.

1

The Long Life of Latin

How many lives can a language have?

Latin is often called a *dead language*, yet it still surprises us with how alive it remains. We no longer hear it in marketplaces or city squares, but it endures in books, in courtrooms, in church liturgy, in science, and in mottos we repeat without even realizing it.

Every time we say *agenda, forum, curriculum,* or *bonus,* we're speaking a little Latin. It's proof that this language doesn't just belong to the past—it keeps living in new forms, quiet but constant.

To call it "dead" is really a paradox. Latin is a language with an extraordinarily long life that, in many ways, has never gone out. Its story began nearly three thousand years ago and stretches across centuries of wars, conquests, art, and culture. To understand where it came from and how it spread is to uncover not just the roots of a language, but also the roots of our identity.

Origins

The story of Latin begins in a specific place: the Palatine Hill, in the heart of Rome. Around 700 BC, what we now see as the cradle of a civilization was then little more than a cluster of wooden and mud huts.

Legend says Rome was founded in 753 BC by twin brothers, Romulus and Remus, sons of the god Mars. The story tells of rivalry, violence, and power: Remus was killed by his brother, and Romulus became the first king of the city that took his name. History or myth, it hardly matters—those dates and tales mark the birth of Rome, and with it, the birth of Latin.

At the time, Latin was spoken by only a few thousand people. It wasn't so different from the sister tongues of nearby regions. The Oscans and Umbrians, for instance, spoke languages so similar that modern linguists group them with Latin under the "Italic languages." They were close relatives, but not identical—something like Italian and Spanish today: partly understandable, yet distinct.

No one back then could have imagined that the speech of a small village would spread far beyond Latium, becoming the voice of an empire and the root of the languages spoken today by hundreds of millions of people.

First Words

Like every language, Latin began as a spoken tongue. For centuries it lived only through the voice—in trade, in prayers to the gods, in military commands. But sooner or later, every growing language finds the need to leave a mark in writing.

For Latin, that moment came early. The first evidence dates to the 6th century BC, not long after the founding of Rome. One of the oldest examples is the famous *Fibula Prenestina*, a golden brooch with a short inscription: *Manios me fhefhaked Numasioi*. It was rough, unpolished Latin with no fixed spelling rules. In its classical form, it would read *Manius me fecit Numerio*—"Manius made me for Numerius."

Another important artifact is a stone from the Roman Forum carved with Latin letters, also dated to the same period. These fragments may be small, but they show that even then Romans had begun to set their language in stone and metal.

The alphabet itself was not a Roman invention. They borrowed it from the Etruscans, who had taken it from the Greeks. From this legacy came the Latin alphabet we still use today—the most widespread writing system in the world.

And it wasn't just letters that traveled. From the Etruscans the Romans absorbed words and ideas as well. Terms like *fenestra* ("window") and *persona* (originally "theatrical mask") reveal the cultural blending that was already shaping Rome's future power.

Empire's Voice

In its early centuries, Rome was only a small kingdom surrounded by larger, stronger peoples, such as the Etruscans to the north. But its strength lay in its ability to grow and integrate. With the fall of the monarchy and the birth of the Republic in 509 BC, Rome began its true expansion.

Wars with neighboring peoples were constant: Latins, Samnites, Etruscans, Sabines. Every victory brought new territory, and with the soldiers came their language. Latin spread not only through conquest—veterans were granted land in conquered regions and settled there with their families. These colonies became pockets of Latin in the middle of other tongues.

Over time, Latin became the language not just of Rome but of the entire peninsula. Instead of dozens of local dialects, it emerged as the common tool for trade, politics, and daily life. Of course, it was not yet uniform. The Latin of farmers in Latium was different from that of generals or senators. But the need to govern wider territories slowly pushed the language toward standardization. Roman speech became a mark of belonging, a shared identity that united diverse peoples.

No one then could have imagined that what began as the dialect of a small village would, within a few centuries, become the language of an empire.

Rome and Greece

Rome knew how to fight, conquer, and govern. But when it came to art, philosophy, and literature, the Romans quickly discovered they had much to learn. The opportunity came with their expansion southward, through the conquest of Magna Graecia and finally Greece itself in the 2nd century BC.

The Romans were captivated by the Greek world—its temples, statues, tragedies, comedies, and philosophy. Confronted with such a refined civilization, they realized that their own language, once used mainly for laws, contracts, and military commands, could also become a medium of art and beauty.

At first, they were mostly imitators. Playwrights like Plautus and Terence adapted Greek models to Roman tastes, bringing to the stage stories and characters born on the shores of the Aegean. Soon after, with Cato the Elder, the first Latin prose texts appeared, such as *De Agri Cultura*. But it was only in the 1st century BC, during the late Republic, that Latin reached full literary maturity. This was the age of Cicero, with his elegant and persuasive prose, and of poets like Virgil, Horace, and Ovid, who raised the language to a refinement equal to Greek.

Thus was born **Classical Latin**—the model that for centuries would be considered the perfect form of the language: a balance of logical rigor and stylistic beauty. From a practical and military tool, Latin had become a language capable of expressing poetry, philosophy, oratory, and art.

Two Latins

While great writers in Rome refined Classical Latin, in the streets and markets the language followed another path. Farmers, soldiers, slaves, and merchants did not speak with the polish of a Cicero or a Horace. They used a Latin that was simpler, more direct, full of abbreviations and local influences. Scholars call this **Vulgar Latin**—the Latin of the people.

The difference between Classical and Vulgar Latin was much like the gap today between literary language and everyday speech. Over time, though, the divide widened. The Roman Empire stretched from Spain to Syria, from North Africa to Gaul, and in every province Latin blended with local dialects.

The result was extraordinary linguistic variety: not one uniform Latin, but many regional Latins. After the fall of the Western Roman Empire in AD 476, as political and administrative structures collapsed, the language lost its unity as well. Provincial Latins slowly evolved into new tongues—the Romance languages: Italian, French, Spanish, Portuguese, and Romanian.

Classical Latin, however, endured as the language of culture, preserved by monks, scholars, and jurists. This created a double legacy: on one hand the modern languages born from Vulgar Latin, and on the other, the "high" Latin that remained for centuries the universal language of European culture.

The Second Life of Latin

With the fall of the Western Roman Empire, Latin did not disappear. On the contrary, it found a new life. It was no longer the everyday speech of the people, which was already evolving into the Romance languages, but it remained the language of culture, faith, and learning.

The Catholic Church adopted it as its official language: Scripture, papal documents, and the liturgy were all in Latin. This ensured that for more than a millennium, Latin stayed alive for anyone who studied, prayed, wrote, or administered.

In medieval universities, Latin was the shared language of students and professors alike. In Bologna as in Paris, in Oxford as in Salamanca, lectures and debates were conducted in Latin—a language that allowed anyone, anywhere in Europe, to understand one another. The same was true in science and philosophy. Landmark works by Thomas Aquinas, Copernicus, Kepler, and Newton were written in Latin, because it was the only truly universal language. Even today, medical, botanical, and legal terminology still carries that imprint.

And centuries later, Latin continues to surprise us. The Vatican still uses it as an official language. Many universities preserve Latin mottos, and we see it in coats of arms, inscriptions, court rulings, and even in everyday expressions. In short, Latin is not a relic of the past but a thread that connects generations—a common heritage that has lived on far longer than the empire that gave it birth.

Why Latin Still Speaks to Us

Centuries later, Latin still speaks. It is not only the root of Italian and the other Romance languages—it shaped our way of thinking, expressing ourselves, and telling the world's stories. Every time we read a Latin motto on a building, a university crest, or a legal ruling, we are reminded that these words have never faded.

Latin has the gift of brevity. With just a few syllables it can hold entire worlds of meaning. Phrases like *Carpe diem* or *Alea iacta est* have crossed millennia and still move us, warn us, and push us to live more fully. This is why Latin is worth approaching. You don't need to be a scholar, nor must you translate entire ancient texts. It is enough to let yourself be inspired by those short, powerful sayings that carry the wisdom of generations.

That is the purpose of this book: to gather 600 Latin quotations, proverbs, and aphorisms for every moment in life. They are phrases to treasure, to draw upon when you need motivation, when you want to surprise in conversation, or simply when you wish to reflect more deeply.

Latin is not dead. It lives in our words, in our thoughts, and in our everyday gestures. It is a quiet companion that has always been with us—and it will continue to be, because while words may fly away, what is written endures: *Verba volant, scripta manent.*

Carpe Diem (1-100)

1.

Carpe diem, quam minimum credula postero.
Seize the day, trust as little as possible in tomorrow.
— Horace, Carmina

2.

Malo periculosam libertatem quam quietum servitium.
I prefer dangerous freedom to quiet slavery.
— Cicero, De officiis

3.

Alea iacta est.
The die is cast.
— Julius Caesar, Crossing the Rubicon

Suetonius tells us that Julius Caesar spoke these words as he led his legions across the Rubicon River, the boundary of Italy at the time: *"The die is cast."* Crossing it meant defying Roman law and starting a civil war—a true point of no return. Today the phrase is still used whenever a decision has been made and there's no turning back.

4.

Fortis fortuna adiuvat.
Fortune favors the bold.
— Terence, Phormio

5.

O tempora, o mores!
Oh, what times! Oh, what morals!
— Cicero, In Catilinam

6.

Nihil est tam fragile quam fama virtutis.
Nothing is so fragile as the reputation of virtue.
— Tacitus, Agricola

7.

(Condicio) sine qua non
Condition without which something cannot exist or occur.
— Common Latin expression

8.

Video meliora proboque, deteriora sequor.
I see and approve the better, but I follow the worse.
— Ovid, Metamorphoses

9.

Rem tene, verba sequentur.
Grasp the subject, the words will follow.
— Cato the Elder (Cato the Censor)

10.

Bis dat qui cito dat.
He gives twice who gives promptly.
— Publilius Syrus, Sententiae

11.

Cynthia prima suis miserum me cepit ocellis.
Cynthia first captured me with her eyes.
— Propertius, Elegiae

12.

Fortunae rota volvitur.
The wheel of fortune turns.
— Medieval proverb (often linked to Boethius, De consolatione
philosophiae)

13.

Homo sum; humani nihil a me alienum puto.
I am human; nothing human is alien to me.
— Terence, Heautontimorumenos

14.

Ubi solitudinem faciunt, pacem appellant.
They make a desert and call it peace.
— Tacitus, Agricola

15.

Homo homini lupus.
Man is a wolf to man.
— Plautus, Asinaria

This famous phrase appears in Plautus (*Asinaria*, 495) and was later taken up and made proverbial by Hobbes in *De Cive* (1651). In antiquity, it expressed the idea that outside the laws and rules of civil society, human beings can become as fierce and dangerous as wild beasts. Today it is used to highlight the harshness of human relationships, conflicts of interest, and the tendency to exploit others when shared values or a regulating authority are absent.

16.

Nulla est enim maior poena quam conscientiae.
There is no greater punishment than conscience.
— Ammianus Marcellinus, Res gestae

17.

Non est ad astra mollis e terris via.
The way from the earth to the stars is not easy.
— Seneca, Hercules Furens

18.

Felix qui potuit rerum cognoscere causas.
Happy is he who has been able to learn the causes of things.
— Virgil, Georgica

19.

Sapere aude.
Dare to know.
— Horace, Epistulae

20.

Vita, si uti scias, longa est.
Life is long if you know how to use it.
— Seneca, De brevitate vitae

21.

Serva me, servabo te.
Save me, and I will save you.
— Petronius, Satyricon

22.

In vino veritas.
In wine, there is truth.
— Pliny the Elder, Naturalis Historia

23.

In principio erat Verbum.
In the beginning was the Word.
— Vulgate, Gospel of John

24.

Memento, homo, quia pulvis es.
Remember, man, that you are dust.
— Vulgate, Genesis

25.

Non nobis solum nati sumus.
We are not born for ourselves alone.
— Cicero, De officiis

26.

Ex tunc.
From the beginning.
— Latin legal expression

27.

Corruptissima re publica plurimae leges.
The more corrupt the state, the more numerous the laws.
— Tacitus, Annales

28.

Non verbis sed factis Deus quaeritur.
God is sought not in words but in deeds.
— St. Jerome, *Commentarius in Epistolam ad Galatas*

29.

Ignoratio Scripturarum ignoratio Christi est.
Ignorance of Scripture is ignorance of Christ.
— St. Jerome, Commentary on Isaiah

30.

Non ducor, duco.
I am not led; I lead.
— Motto of São Paulo, Brazil

31.

Audentes fortuna iuvat.
Fortune favors the bold.
— Vergil, Aeneis

32.

Gutta cavat lapidem.
A drop hollows a stone.
— Ovid, Epistulae ex Ponto

33.

Omnis creatura in Deo fulget.
Every creature shines in God.
— Pope Francis, Laudato Si'

34.

Quo usque tandem abutere, Catilina, patientia nostra?
How long, Catiline, will you abuse our patience?
— Cicero, In Catilinam

35.

Quidquid agis, prudenter agas et respice finem.
Whatever you do, do it wisely and consider the end.
— Publilius Syrus, Sententiae

36.

Amicitia nisi inter bonos esse non potest.

Friendship cannot exist except among the good.
— Cicero, Laelius de amicitia

37.

Pacta sunt servanda.

Agreements must be kept.
— Roman legal maxim

38.

Nemo iudex in causa sua.

No one is judge in his own case.
— Roman legal maxim

39.

Non est ad astra mollis e terris via.

There is no easy way from the earth to the stars.
— Seneca, Hercules Furens

40.

Natura, non ars, facit poetam.

It is nature, not art, that makes a poet.
— Quintilian, Institutio oratoria

41.

Nemo tenetur se ipsum accusare.

No one is bound to accuse himself.
— Principle of the right to silence

42.

Dum spiro, spero.
While I breathe, I hope.
— Cicero, attributed

43.

Labor omnia vincit improbus.
Steady work conquers all things.
— Virgil, Georgica

44.

Sic transit gloria mundi.
Thus passes the glory of the world.
— Medieval saying, used in papal coronations

"Thus passes the glory of the world" —a phrase that sounds like an eternal warning. Born as a medieval liturgical formula, it was pronounced during the coronation of popes to remind them that, despite the honor and power they had just received, all earthly things are destined to fade. It is a reflection on the transience of life and fame, fitting to underscore the fragility of human achievements and the vanity of those who believe they can last forever. Used today in conversation or in writing, it retains its full force: it invites us to look at both success and failure with perspective, reminding us that nothing lasts forever.

45.

Amor tussisque non celatur.
Love and a cough cannot be concealed.
— Latin proverb

46.

Mens sana in corpore sano.
A sound mind in a sound body.
— Juvenal, Satirae

47.

Cave ne cadas.
Take care not to fall.
— Latin proverbial warning

48.

Cum tacent, clamant.
By keeping silent, they cry out.
— Cicero, Pro Milone

49.

Historia magistra vitae.
History is the teacher of life.
— Cicero, De oratore

50.

Omnium rerum principia parva sunt.
The beginnings of all things are small.
— Cicero, De finibus

51.

Magna imperia gravibus periculis clarescunt.
Great powers shine forth through great dangers.
— Velleius Paterculus, Historiae Romanae

52.

Aut vincere aut mori.
Either to conquer or to die.
— Latin military motto

53.

Accipe quam primum.
Accept as soon as possible.
— Latin proverb

54.

Per aspera ad astra.
Through hardships to the stars.
— Seneca, Hercules Furens

55.

Natura nihil frustra facit.
Nature does nothing in vain.
— Aristotle, De caelo (Greek maxim in Latin form)

56.

Cui bono?
Who benefits?
— Cicero, Pro Roscio Amerino

57.

Fortuna caeca est.
Fortune is blind.
— Cicero, Tusculanae disputationes

58.

Victrix causa deis placuit, sed victa Catoni.
The victorious cause pleased the gods, but the defeated one pleased Cato.
— Lucan, Pharsalia

59.

Probitas laudatur et alget.
Honesty is praised, and yet it freezes.
— Juvenal, Satirae

60.

Pecunia non olet.
Money does not smell.
— Suetonius, Vespasianus

61.

Quis custodiet ipsos custodes?
Who will guard the guards themselves?
— Juvenal, Satirae

This famous maxim from Juvenal highlights an eternal problem: who controls the controllers? In its original context it referred to marital fidelity, but over time its meaning broadened to issues of power and the need to limit it. Today it is used in politics, law, and even technology to point out the risk of corruption and the lack of transparency in systems of oversight.

62.

Miser est qui se ipsum ignorat.
Unhappy is he who does not know himself.
— Apuleius, Florida

63.

Si vis amari, ama.
If you wish to be loved, love.
— Seneca, Epistulae morales

64.

Experientia magistra rerum.
Experience is the teacher of all things.
— Cicero, De oratore

65.

Mors certa, hora incerta.
Death is certain, the hour is uncertain.
— Medieval saying

66.

Acta est fabula.
The play is ended.
— Suetonius, Augustus

67.

Honeste vivere, alterum non laedere, suum cuique tribuere.
To live honorably, not to injure another, to give each his due.
— Ulpian, Digesta

68.

Silentium est aureum.
Silence is golden.
— Medieval Latin proverb

69.

Vox populi, vox Dei.
The voice of the people is the voice of God.
— Alcuin, Epistulae

70.

Nullum magnum ingenium sine mixtura dementiae fuit.
There has never been a great genius without a touch of madness.
— Seneca, De tranquillitate animi

71.

Nihil est tam naturale quam senescere.
Nothing is so natural as growing old.
— Pliny the Younger, Epistulae

72.

Fiat voluntas tua.
Thy will be done.
— Vulgate, Gospel of Matthew

73.

Homo totiens moritur quoties amittit suos.
A man dies as many times as he loses his loved ones.
— Apuleius, Metamorphoses

74.

Verba volant, scripta manent.
Spoken words fly away, written words endure.
— Seneca, Epistulae morales

75.

Fructum non fert terra, nisi cultura adiuvetur.
The land bears no fruit unless cultivation aids it.
— Columella, De Re Rustica

76.

Cuius regio, eius religio.
Whose realm, his religion.
— Legal formula, Peace of Augsburg

This is not an ancient motto but a political formula from the 16th century, established with the Peace of Augsburg (1555) to settle religious conflicts in Germany. It declared that every subject had to follow the religion of his ruler: Catholicism or Lutheranism, depending on the case. Today, the expression is used to indicate the close connection between political power and religion, or more generally to highlight how the values and rules of those in power inevitably shape the lives of those they govern.

77.

Non scholae, sed vitae discimus.
We do not learn for school, but for life.
— Seneca, Epistulae morales

78.

Dum Romae consulitur, Saguntum expugnatur.
While Rome debates, Saguntum is taken.
— Livy, Ab urbe condita

79.

Virtus numquam perit.
Virtue never perishes.
— Claudian, In Rufinum

80.

Nemo nascitur sapiens.
No one is born wise.
— Seneca, Epistulae morales

81.

Nihil est dulcius quam verum dicere.
Nothing is sweeter than to speak the truth.
— Fronto, Epistulae ad Marcum Caesarem

82.

Nemo iudex in causa sua.
No one is judge in his own case.
— Roman legal maxim

83.

Amor vincit omnia.
Love conquers all.
— Virgil, Eclogae

84.

Ignis aurum probat, miseria fortes viros.
Fire tests gold, adversity tests strong men.
— Seneca, De providentia

85.

Mors ultima linea rerum est.
Death is the final limit of things.
— Horace, Epistulae

86.

Docendo discimus.
By teaching, we learn.
— Seneca, Epistulae morales

87.

Cuiusvis hominis est errare, nullius nisi insipientis perseverare in errore.
To err is human, but only a fool persists in error.
— Cicero, Philippicae

88.

Primum non nocere.
First, do no harm.
— Attributed to Hippocrates, medieval medical tradition

89.

Modus operandi
Method of operating or acting.
— Common Latin expression

90.

Lux in is lucet.
The light shines in the darkness.
— Vulgate, Gospel of John

91.

Inopiae desunt multa, avaritiae omnia.

Poverty lacks many things, greed lacks everything.
— Juvenal, Satirae

92.

Nemo est tam senex qui se annum non putet posse vivere.

No man is so old that he does not think he can live another year.
— Cornelius Nepos, Cato

93.

Nihil est ab omni parte beatum.

Nothing is happy in every respect.
— Martial, Epigrammata

94.

Caritas omnia suffert.

Love bears all things.
— Vulgate, First Epistle to the Corinthians

95.

Audere est facere.

To dare is to do.
— Latin proverb

96.

Fiat iustitia, pereat mundus.

Let justice be done, though the world perish.
— Medieval legal proverb

97.

Dura lex, sed lex.
The law is harsh, but it is the law.
— Latin proverb, attributed to Ulpian

"The law is harsh, but it is the law" —a proverb traced back to the Roman jurist Ulpian that reflects the realistic spirit of Roman law. Laws may seem severe, at times even unjust in their rigidity, yet they must be respected because they guarantee order and civil coexistence. It reminds us that no society can endure without common norms, and that respect for the law is the very foundation of justice.

98.

Si fallor, sum.
If I am mistaken, I exist.
— Augustine, De Civitate Dei

99.

Nulla salus bello.
No safety comes from war.
— Ovid, Metamorphoses

100.

Cor ad cor loquitur.
Heart speaks to heart.
— John Henry Newman, modern Latin motto

Hic et Nunc (101 – 200)

101.

Malum est consilium quod mutari non potest.
Evil is the plan that cannot be changed.
— Publilius Syrus, Sententiae

102.

Aliud est theoria, aliud usus.
One thing is theory, another is practice.
— Latin proverb

103.

Res, non verba.
Deeds, not words.
— Latin proverb

104.

Fortuna fortes metuit, ignavos premit.
Fortune fears the brave and crushes the cowardly.
— Seneca, Epistulae Morales ad Lucilium

105.

Amicitiae nostrae memoriam spero sempiternam fore.
I hope the memory of our friendship will be eternal.
— Cicero, Epistulae ad Atticum

106.

Vitam regit fortuna, non sapientia.
Life is ruled by chance, not by wisdom.
— Cicero, Tusculanae disputationes

107.

Maior est virtus quam felicitas.
Virtue is greater than good fortune.
— Curtius Rufus, Historiae Alexandri

108.

Virtus ipsa pretium est.
Virtue is its own reward.
— Cicero, Philippicae

109.

Audiatur et altera pars.
Let the other side be heard as well.
— Seneca, De beneficiis

110.

Homo homini res sacra est.
Man is sacred to man.
— Publilius Syrus, Sententiae

111.

Nulla tenaci invia est via.
No road is impassable to the persistent.
— Latin proverb

112.

Veritas filia temporis.
Truth is the daughter of time.
— Aulus Gellius, Noctes Atticae

113.

Naturam expellas furca, tamen usque recurret.
Drive nature out with a pitchfork, yet she will always return.
— Horace, Epistulae

114.

Ars est celare artem.
True art is to conceal art.
— Ovid, Ars amatoria

"Art lies in concealing art": a saying that may sound like a paradox, yet it holds a universal truth. The true artist does not display the effort, only the result; perfection appears natural, spontaneous, almost inevitable. Born in the world of rhetoric and later extended to all the arts, this maxim reminds us that the finest technique is the one that remains invisible, allowing only the beauty of the work to shine through. Today it can be used to highlight how behind apparent simplicity often lies great labor—whether in a well-crafted speech, a flawless performance, or a simple gesture of elegance.

115.

Nunc est bibendum.
Now is the time to drink.
— Horace, Carmina

116.

Quod licet Iovi, non licet bovi.
What is permitted to Jupiter is not permitted to the ox.
— Latin proverb

117.

Nec spe nec metu.
Neither with hope nor with fear.
— Motto, Seneca

118.

Non multa sed multum.

Not many things, but much in depth.
— Pliny the Younger, Epistulae

119.

Nemo me lacrimis decoret nec funera fletu faxit.

Let no one honor me with tears, nor make my funeral with weeping.
— Ennius, Annales

120.

Fata viam invenient.

The Fates will find a way.
— Virgil, Aeneis

121.

Caelum non animum mutant qui trans mare currunt.

They change their sky, not their soul, who cross the sea.
— Horace, Epistulae

122.

Sic semper tyrannis.

Thus always to tyrants.
— Motto of Virginia

123.

Cave canem.

Beware of the dog.
— Pompeian mosaic

124.

Qui transtulit sustinet.
He who transplanted still sustains.
— Motto of Connecticut

125.

Spes addita firmat animum.
Added hope strengthens the spirit.
— Silius Italicus, Punica

126.

Omne initium difficile est.
Every beginning is difficult.
— Latin proverb

127.

Amor magister optimus.
Love is the best teacher.
— Latin proverb

128.

Tempora mutantur et nos mutamur in illis.
Times change, and we change with them.
— Medieval Latin proverb

129.

Finis coronat opus.
The end crowns the work.
— Ovid, Heroides

130.

Qui ridet ultimus, longe est qui ridet optime.
He who laughs last, laughs best.
— Martial, Epigrammata

131.

Nemo est supra leges.
No one is above the law.
— Roman legal maxim

132.

Legum servi sumus ut liberi esse possimus.
We are servants of the laws so that we may be free.
— Cicero, Pro Cluentio

133.

Nemo propheta in patria.
No one is a prophet in his own land.
— Vulgate, Gospel of Luke

134.

Amicus certus in re incerta cernitur.
A true friend is recognized in times of difficulty.
— Cicero, De amicitia

135.

Audi alteram partem.
Hear the other side.
— Roman legal maxim

136.

Qui tacet consentire videtur.

Silence gives consent.
— Medieval legal maxim

137.

Natura non facit saltus.

Nature does not make leaps.
— Latin proverb, later taken up by Linnaeus

This maxim expresses the idea of continuity in natural processes. Nothing in nature happens all at once, without intermediate steps; every transformation is slow, gradual, and the result of a path. This expression, already present in Aristotelian thought and later taken up in Latin tradition, eventually became a fundamental principle in science and philosophy, appearing even in the works of Leibniz and Darwin. Today it reminds us that change—whether in life, study, or work—requires time and patience: no true achievement comes suddenly, but is always the fruit of steady evolution.

138.

Dominus vobiscum.

The Lord be with you.
— Catholic liturgy, Mass

139.

Magnitudo animi in tolerando est.

Greatness of spirit lies in endurance.
— Seneca, De vita beata

140.

Contra spem spero.
I hope against all hope.
— Vulgate, Epistula ad Romanos

141.

Historia testis temporum, lux veritatis, vita memoriae, magistra vitae.
History is the witness of time, the light of truth, the life of memory, the teacher of life.
— Velleius Paterculus, Historia Romana

142.

Da mi basia mille, deinde centum.
Give me a thousand kisses, then a hundred.
— Catullus, Carmina

143.

Omnes homines natura aequales sunt.
All men are equal by nature.
— Ulpian, Digest

144.

Salus populi suprema lex esto.
The welfare of the people shall be the supreme law.
— Cicero, De legibus

145.

In nomine Patris, et Filii, et Spiritus Sancti.
In the name of the Father, and of the Son, and of the Holy Spirit.
— Christian liturgical formula

146.

Pueri pueri, puerilia tractant.
Children are children, and deal with childish things.
— Latin proverb

147.

Vincit qui se vincit.
He conquers who conquers himself.
— Seneca, Epistulae morales

148.

Stat magni nominis umbra.
Only the shadow of a great name remains.
— Lucan, Pharsalia

149.

Bonis nocet quisquis pepercit malis.
He who spares the wicked harms the good.
— Publilius Syrus, Sententiae

150.

Lex posterior derogat priori.
The later law repeals the earlier one.
— Roman legal maxim

151.

Diligentia maximum etiam mediocritatem transcendit.
Diligence surpasses even the greatest mediocrity.
— Cicero, De officiis

152.

Sapientis est mutare consilium.

It is the mark of a wise man to change his mind.
— Seneca, Epistulae morales

153.

Satis est, si unum bene colas agrum.

It is enough to cultivate even a single field well.
— Columella, De re rustica

154.

Ignis necavit multos, sed fames plurimos.

Fire has killed many, but hunger far more.
— Seneca, Epistulae morales

155.

Legere est agere.

To read is to act.
— Latin proverb

156.

Lux mea lex.

My light is my law.
— Medieval Latin motto

157.

Natura duce, numquam aberrabis.

With nature as your guide, you will never go astray.
— Seneca, Epistulae morales

158.

Plures efficimur, quoties metimur a vobis: semen est sanguis Christianorum.
We grow in number every time you mow us down: the blood of Christians is seed.
— Tertullian, Apologeticum

159.

Inquietum est cor nostrum, donec requiescat in Te.
Our heart is restless until it rests in You.
— Augustine, Confessiones

160.

Ars gratia artis.
Art for the sake of art.
— Modern Latin motto

161.

Hic et nunc.
Here and now.
— Latin proverb

162.

Memoria minuitur nisi eam exerceas.
Memory fades unless you exercise it.
— Cicero, Tusculanae disputationes

163.

Mors certa, vita incerta.
Death is certain, life is uncertain.
— Latin proverb

164.

Nemo malus felix.
No wicked man is happy.
— Cicero, Tusculanae disputationes

165.

Non possumus.
We cannot.
— Vulgate, Acts of the Apostles

166.

Omnia tempus habent.
Everything has its time.
— Vulgate, Ecclesiastes

167.

Repetita iuvant.
Repetition is useful.
— Latin proverb

168.

Sapientia prima est stultitia caruisse.
The first step to wisdom is to be free from folly.
— Horace, Epistulae

169.

Satius est supervacua scire quam nihil.
It is better to know useless things than to know nothing.
— Seneca, Epistulae morales

170.

Scientia potentia est.
Knowledge is power.
— Bacon, rendered in Latin

171.

Ubi bene, ibi patria.
Where one feels good, there is one's homeland.
— Cicero, Tusculanae disputationes

172.

Unus pro omnibus, omnes pro uno.
One for all, all for one.
— Medieval Latin motto

173.

Verba docent, exempla trahunt.
Words instruct, examples lead.
— Latin proverb

174.

In fraudem legis.
In fraud of the law.
— Latin legal expression

175.

Volenti non fit iniuria.
No injustice is done to one who consents.
— Ulpian, Digesta

176.

Natura artis magistra.
Nature is the teacher of art.
— Cicero, De natura deorum

This saying highlights how every human creation, no matter how refined, always draws inspiration from the perfection of nature. Ancient artists looked to the world around them as the truest source of beauty and harmony. Even today, the maxim invites us to observe our surroundings and learn from them: in the shape of a leaf, the proportions of a body, or the simplicity of a landscape, we find the highest lesson of balance and creativity. It is a motto that reminds us how inseparable art and nature are, and how each continues to nourish the other.

177.

Nulli tacuisse nocet, nocet esse locutum.
Silence has never harmed anyone; speaking has.
— Petronius, Satyricon

178.

Fides vincit impetum furoris.
Faith conquers the onrush of madness.
— Prudentius, Psychomachia

179.

Omnia mutantur, nihil interit.
Everything changes, nothing perishes.
— Ovid, Metamorphoses

180.

Peccavi.
I have sinned.
— Vulgate, Numbers

181.

Eloquentia nisi ad virtutem referatur, malum est.
Eloquence, if not directed toward virtue, is a vice.
— Fronto, Epistulae ad Antoninum Pium

182.

Moribus antiquis res stat Romana virisque.
The strength of Rome rests on ancient customs and men.
— Ennius, Annales

183.

Porta patet, cor magis.
The door is open, the heart even more so.
— Medieval Latin hospitable motto

184.

Fama crescit eundo.
Fame grows as it goes.
— Aulus Gellius, Noctes Atticae

185.

Pulchrum est bene facere rei publicae, etiam bene dicere haud absurdum est.
It is noble to act well for the republic, and not without value to speak well of it too.
— Sallust, Bellum Catilinae

186.

Principiis obsta.
Resist beginnings (stop evils at their first appearance).
— Ovid, Remedia amoris

187.

Iustitia fundamentum regnorum est.
Justice is the foundation of kingdoms.
— Cassiodorus, Variae

188.

Qui bene amat, bene castigat.
He who loves well, chastises well.
— Latin proverb

189.

Quo semel est imbuta recens servabit odorem testa diu.
A fresh jar will long preserve the scent of what it was first soaked in.
— Horace, Epistulae

190.

Repetitio est mater studiorum.
Repetition is the mother of learning.
— Latin proverb

191.

Roma caput mundi.
Rome, the center of the world.
— Roman motto

192.

Roma locuta, causa finita.
Rome has spoken, the case is closed.
— Augustine, Sermones

193.

Hic et ubique terrarum
Here and everywhere on Earth.
— University of Paris (Sorbonne)

194.

Amantium irae amoris integratio est.
The quarrels of lovers are the renewal of love.
— Plautus, Andria

195.

Similia similibus curantur.
Like is cured by like.
— Hippocrates, later adopted by Samuel Hahnemann

196.

Stultorum plena sunt omnia.
The world is full of fools.
— Cicero, Tusculanae disputationes

197.

Sub specie aeternitatis.
Under the aspect of eternity.
— Latin philosophical concept

198.

Suum cuique.
To each his own.
— Ulpian, Digesta

199.

Tertium non datur.
No third is given (no third possibility exists).
— Aristotle, Organon, Latin formulation

This expression comes from Aristotelian logic and refers to the so-called law of the excluded middle. Put simply, it means that between two opposing alternatives there is no third way: something is either true or false; no other option exists. Over time, the formula moved beyond philosophy to become a motto of clarity and decisiveness. To use it today is to say that we cannot always hide in nuances: in certain cases, we must choose, without half-measures.

200.

Veritas odium parit.
Truth breeds hatred.
— Terence, Andria

Nomen Omen (201 – 300)

201.

Tam mala sunt vicina quam proxima.
Neighbors are as troublesome as close relatives.
— Martial, Epigrammata

202.

Legere est non verba sed sensus haurire.
To read is not to absorb words, but meanings.
— Isidore of Seville, Etymologiae

203.

Bellum se ipsum alet.
War feeds itself.
— Livy, Ab urbe condita

204.

Clavus clavo pellitur.
One nail drives out another.
— Cicero, Tusculanae disputationes

205.

Ex nihilo nihil fit.
Nothing comes from nothing.
— Lucretius, De rerum natura

This maxim is one of the oldest principles of Western thought. It appears in the work of Lucretius but was already present in earlier Greek philosophy, especially in Parmenides. The idea is that no thing can arise out of absolute nothingness; everything must come from something that already exists. In antiquity, this was a way to explain natural phenomena without invoking supernatural creation. Over time, the maxim has influenced both scientific reasoning and theological debates, becoming a shorthand for the principle of causality. Today, it is still quoted whenever we want to stress that results, events, or achievements cannot appear without a cause or an effort.

206.

Felix culpa.
Happy fault.
— Augustine, Enchiridion

207.

Hostis hosti crudelis.
An enemy is cruel to his enemy.
— Latin proverb

208.

Gaudeamus igitur.
Therefore, let us rejoice.
— Medieval student hymn

209.

Gutta cavat lapidem non vi sed saepe cadendo.
The drop hollows the stone not by force, but by falling often.
— Ovid, Epistulae ex Ponto

210.

Hic Rhodus, hic salta.
Here is Rhodes, jump here.
— Aesop, Greek maxim in Latin form

This phrase comes from a fable by Aesop, later taken up by Marx, and it ridicules those who boast of extraordinary feats never proven. In the story, a man claimed he had made an incredible jump in Rhodes; he was told, "Here is Rhodes, jump here!" The meaning is clear: enough words, prove now what you say. Today it is used as an invitation to immediate action, to expose those who promise much but do not act, or to encourage someone to seriously test their abilities. It is a direct, pragmatic motto that reminds us that deeds matter more than words.

211.

Fiat iustitia, ruat caelum.
Let justice be done, though the heavens fall.
— Medieval legal maxim

212.

Ignorantia legis non excusat.
Ignorance of the law excuses no one.
— Roman legal maxim

213.

Parentes colendos esse.
Parents must be honored.
— Latin maxim

214.

In dubio pro reo.
When in doubt, for the accused.
— Roman legal maxim

215.

Inter arma silent leges.
In times of war, the laws fall silent.
— Cicero, Pro Milone

216.

Factum est illud, fieri infectum non potest.
What is done cannot be undone.
— Plautus, Trinummus

217.

Littera scripta manet.
The written word remains.
— Cicero, Epistulae ad familiares

218.

Magna est vis consuetudinis.
Great is the power of habit.
— Cicero, De finibus

219.

Medicus curat, natura sanat.
The doctor treats, nature heals.
— Latin proverb

220.

Mens agitat molem.
The mind moves the mass.
— Virgil, Aeneid

221.

Mundus vult decipi, ergo decipiatur.
The world wants to be deceived, therefore let it be deceived.
— Medieval Latin proverb

222.

Fortuna vitrea est: tum cum splendet frangitur.
Fortune is glass: just when it shines, it breaks.
— Publilius Syrus, Sententiae

223.

Nemo saltat sobrius.
No one dances sober.
— Cicero, Pro Murena

224.

Nihil sub sole novum.
There is nothing new under the sun.
— Vulgate, Ecclesiastes

225.

Nomen omen.
The name is an omen.
— Plautus, Persa

"The name is an omen": a short and striking Latin formula that conveys the idea that a person's destiny is hidden in their name. The Romans already believed that names were not accidental but carried a deep, almost prophetic meaning. A surname or a nickname could thus become a clue to one's character or future. Today, this expression is often used in an ironic or playful way, when someone's name really seems to reflect their personality or profession. It is a motto that, in just a few words, combines the charm of antiquity with the lightness of modern life.

226.

Quam miserum est, cum se renovat miseria!
How wretched it is when misfortune returns!
— Publilius Syrus, Sententiae

227.

Nulla est celeritate virtus aeque laudanda.
No virtue is to be praised as much as speed.
— Cornelius Nepos, Miltiades

228.

Nullum crimen sine lege.
No crime without a law.
— Roman legal maxim

229.

Nemo est dignus imperio nisi qui se ipse regere potest.
No one is worthy of command unless he can govern himself.
— Curtius Rufus, Historiae Alexandri

230.

Animus hominis est supra omnia.
The spirit of man is above all things.
— Latin proverb

231.

Dei sub numine viget.
Under God's power she flourishes.
— Motto of Princeton University

232.

Parva scintilla saepe magnam flamman excitat.
A small spark often kindles a great flame.
— Latin proverb

233.

Pater patriae.
Father of the fatherland.
— Livy, Ab urbe condita

234.

Paupertas onus est.
Poverty is a burden.
— Seneca, Epistulae morales

235.

Periculum est in mora.
There is danger in delay.
— Livy, Ab urbe condita

236.

Primum vivere, deinde philosophari.
First live, then philosophize.
— Latin proverb

237.

Quae nocent, docent.
What harms, teaches.
— Latin proverb

238.

Quamdiu se bene gesserit.
As long as he shall have behaved well.
— Latin legal maxim

239.

Quod erat demonstrandum.
Which was to be demonstrated.
— Euclid, Latin formula

240.

Quod scripsi, scripsi.
What I have written, I have written.
— Vulgate, Gospel of John

241.

Quis fuit horrendos primus qui protulit enses?
Who was the first to draw the dreadful swords?
— Tibullus, Elegiae

242.

Ubi societas, ibi ius.
Where there is society, there is law.
— Roman legal proverb

243.

Sapientia est potentia.
Knowledge is power.
— Latin proverb

244.

Si vis pacem, para bellum.
If you want peace, prepare for war.
— Vegetius, Epitoma rei militaris

245.

Animus in consulendo liber
A mind unfettered in deliberation.
— NATO (North Atlantic Treaty Organization)

246.

Spes ultima dea.
Hope is the last goddess.
— Latin proverb

247.

Stella duce.
With the star as guide.
— Christian Latin motto

248.

Suaviter in modo, fortiter in re.
Gentle in manner, strong in action.
— Cicero, De officiis

249.

Tantum religio potuit suadere malorum.
So great the evils religion could persuade.
— Lucretius, De rerum natura

250.

Ubi caritas et amor, Deus ibi est.
Where charity and love are, there is God.
— Latin liturgical hymn

251.

Ubi maior, minor cessat.
Where the greater is, the lesser yields.
— Latin proverb

This Latin maxim reflects a principle of hierarchy: when two authorities, arguments, or forces come into conflict, the stronger or more important one prevails, and the weaker must give way. The expression was widely used in legal and rhetorical contexts to indicate precedence and order, but it also became a common proverb in everyday life. Today it is still cited to underline the idea that, in any situation, the greater authority, power, or reason overrides the lesser.

252.

Ubi concordia, ibi victoria.
Where there is harmony, there is victory.
— Latin proverb

253.

Ultima ratio regum.
The final argument of kings.
— Inscription on the artillery of Louis XIV

254.

Una hirundo non facit ver.
One swallow does not make spring.
— Aristotle, Latin tradition

255.

Unusquisque faber est fortunae suae.
Every man is the architect of his own fortune.
— Appius Claudius Caecus, Sententiae

256.

Ut sementem feceris, ita metes.
As you sow, so shall you reap.
— Cicero, Philippicae

257.

Vacare culpa magnum est solacium.
To be free from guilt is a great comfort.
— Seneca, Epistulae morales

258.

Vae victis.
Woe to the vanquished.
— Livy, Ab urbe condita

259.

In hoc signo vinces.
In this sign, you will conquer.
— Christian tradition, Vision of Constantine

260.

Varium et mutabile semper femina.
Woman is ever fickle and changeable.
— Virgil, Aeneid

261.

Verba volant, scripta manent.
Spoken words fly away, written ones remain.
— Latin proverb

262.

Veritas numquam perit.
Truth never perishes.
— Seneca, Epistulae morales

263.

Quis fuit primus qui protulit enses?
Who was the first to draw the dreadful swords?
— Tibullus, Elegiae

264.

Vincit omnia veritas.
Truth conquers all.
— Latin proverb

265.

Vir bonus dicendi peritus.
An honest man, skilled in speaking.
— Cicero, De oratore

266.

Virtus et scientia.
Virtue and knowledge.
— Latin university motto

267.

Vita mutatur, non tollitur.
Life is changed, not ended.
— Latin liturgy

268.

Vita sine libertate nihil.
Life without liberty is nothing.
— Latin proverb

269.

Vitam impendere vero.
To devote life to truth.
— Juvenal, Satires

270.

Vivamus, mea Lesbia, atque amemus.
Let us live, my Lesbia, and let us love.
— Catullus, Carmina

271.

Vivo ut vivas.
I live so that you may live.
— Latin proverb

272.

Vultus est index animi.
The face is the mirror of the soul.
— Cicero, De officiis

273.

Vulgus vult decipi.
The crowd wishes to be deceived.
— Latin proverb

This maxim is traditionally attributed to Petronius and, in some variants, also to other late–antique authors. It is not so much an insult to the people as a bitter observation: the masses often prefer comforting illusions to the truth, which may be uncomfortable or painful. Over the centuries, the expression has been echoed in political and religious contexts to stress how easily crowds can be manipulated with promises, spectacles, or convenient beliefs. Today, it is used to describe—often with a critical or ironic tone—the collective tendency to be guided more by appearances than by reality.

274.

Ab imo pectore.
From the depths of the heart.
— Cicero, Epistulae ad Atticum

275.

Ab initio.
From the beginning.
— Latin expression

276.

Ab uno disce omnes.
From one, learn all.
— Virgil, Aeneid

277.

Fortuna multis dat nimium, nulli .
Fortune gives too much to many, to none enough.
— Martial, Epigrammata

278.

Ad astra per aspera.
To the stars through difficulties.
— Seneca, Hercules furens

279.

Ad kalendas Graecas.
At the Greek Kalends (never).
— Suetonius, Augustus

This Latin maxim comes from Roman times and was already a proverbial expression of impossibility. The Romans had "*Kalends*," the first day of the month, but the Greeks did not — so to postpone something "*to the Greek Kalends*" meant to postpone it forever, to a date that would never come. Suetonius records that Emperor Augustus often used the phrase when referring to bad debtors who promised payment but never intended to pay. Today, the maxim is used ironically to indicate that something will never happen, much like saying "*when pigs fly.*"

280.

Ad maiora.
Toward greater things.
— Latin augural formula

281.

Ad multos annos.
For many years.
— Latin augural formula

282.

Ad perpetuam rei memoriam.
To the perpetual memory of the matter.
— Latin ecclesiastical formula

283.

Ad usum Delphini.
For the use of the Dauphin.
— French Latin editions

284.

Ad vitam aeternam.
For eternal life.
— Latin liturgical formula

285.

Ad vitam paramus.
We prepare for life.
— Latin proverb

286.

Age quod agis.
Do what you are doing.
— Latin proverb

287.

Agnosce te, o homo.
Recognize yourself, O man.
— Christian Latin proverb

288.

Amor caecus est.
Love is blind.
— Latin proverb

This Latin proverb needs little explanation. The Romans already
recognized that those who love often fail to see the flaws of the
beloved, or let themselves be carried away by passions that cloud
judgment. The image of blind love has enjoyed a long tradition
in literature, from antiquity to Shakespeare, and it has become
a universal way to describe the irrational power of love. Today
it is used to comment—sometimes with irony, sometimes with
tenderness—on the behavior of those who, in love, seem to lose all
critical sense.

289.

Amor vincit mortem.
Love conquers death.
— Christian Latin proverb

290.

Amor verus numquam moritur.
True love never dies.
— Latin proverb

291.

Amor vitae.
Love of life.
— Latin motto

292.

Amoris vulnus idem sanat qui facit.
The wound of love is healed by the one who made it.
— Publilius Syrus, Sententiae

293.

Amplius semper cupientes.
Always desiring more.
— Latin proverb

294.

Anima candida.
Pure soul.
— Latin motto

295.

Anima mea in manibus meis semper.
My soul is always in my hands.
— Vulgate, Psalmus

296.

Animi causa.
For the sake of the spirit.
— Latin proverb

297.

Aqua et igni interdictus.
Deprived of water and fire (banishment).
— Roman legal maxim

298.

Aquila non capit muscas.
The eagle does not catch flies.
— Latin proverb

This quote conveys the idea that great people, powers, or minds should not waste time on trivial matters. In Roman culture, the eagle symbolized strength and authority, so to say that an eagle ignores flies was to stress dignity and focus on what truly matters. Over the centuries, the proverb has been used to advise against pettiness, quarrels, or distractions, reminding us that those who aim high should not be bothered by insignificant things. Today it is often quoted in the same sense: don't stoop to trivialities when your goals are greater.

299.

Arbor vitae.
Tree of life.
— Vulgate, Genesis

300.

Arcana imperii.
Secrets of power.
— Tacitus, Historiae

5

Cogito Ergo Sum (301 – 400)

301.

Corpus delicti.
The body of the crime.
— Latin legal maxim

302.

Amicitia non debet violari, nisi propter culpam.
Friendship should not be broken except for serious fault.
— Cornelius Nepos, Atticus

303.

Cogito, ergo sum.
I think, therefore I am.
— Descartes, Meditations (Latin formulation)

304.

Habeas corpus
You shall have the body.
— Latin legal formula (English constitutional law)

This principle is one of the cornerstones of Anglo-American law. The phrase literally means that the detained person must be *"brought before the court."* It first emerged in medieval England as a safeguard against arbitrary imprisonment and later became a constitutional right in both Britain and the United States. The writ of habeas corpus allows a judge to review whether a person is being held lawfully and ensures that no one can be jailed without due process. Over centuries, it has come to symbolize personal freedom and legal protection against abuse of power, and it is still invoked today in cases of unlawful detention.

305.

Celerius quam asparagi coquantur.
Faster than asparagus cooks.
— Suetonius, Augustus

306.

Consuetudo est altera natura.
Habit is a second nature.
— Cicero, De finibus

307.

E pluribus unum.
Out of many, one.
— Motto of the United States (1782)

308.

Beata solitudo, sola beatitudo.
Blessed solitude, the only happiness.
— Monastic proverb

309.

Contra principia negantem non est disputandum.
There can be no debate with someone who denies first principles.
— Aristotle (Latin formulation)

310.

Caeca invidia est.
Envy is blind.
— Livy, Ab urbe condita

311.

Capax infiniti.
Capable of the infinite.
— Augustine, Confessiones

312.

Curriculum vitae.
Course of life.
— Latin expression

313.

Cuique suum.
To each his own.
— Latin legal maxim

314.

Calamitas virtutis occasio est.
Calamity is an opportunity for virtue.
— Seneca, De providentia

315.

Nullum crimen, nulla poena sine lege.
No crime, no punishment without law.
— Latin legal maxim, principle of legality

316.

Brevior via est multum properantis errare.
The shorter way is for the one who hurries too much to go astray.
— Seneca, Epistulae morales

317.

Castigat ridendo mores.
Customs are corrected by laughing.
— Latin theatrical proverb

318.

Ars amandi.
The art of loving.
— Ovid, Ars amatoria

319.

Caveat emptor.
Let the buyer beware.
— Latin legal maxim

320.

Nemo repente fit turpissimus.
No one becomes utterly wicked all at once.
— Petronius, Satyricon

321.

Audi, vide, tace.
Listen, observe, and be silent.
— Latin proverb

This lapidary motto is often extended with *si vis vivere in pace* — *"if you want to live in peace."* The advice is straightforward: before speaking, it is wiser to listen carefully and observe, since silence often leads to serenity and prudence. In antiquity, it worked both as practical wisdom and as political caution: those who knew how to remain silent were less exposed to the dangers of power. Today, the phrase is still relevant — it can be used to recommend discretion, highlight the value of listening, or simply as a timeless rule for living peacefully with others.

322.

Crux fidelis.
Faithful cross.
— Latin liturgical hymn

323.

Cedant arma togae.
Let arms yield to the toga.
— Cicero, De officiis

324.

Castus morum.
Guardian of morals.
— Latin expression

325.

Nihil est tam fragile quam fama potentiae non sua vi nixa.
Nothing is as fragile as the reputation of power not supported by its own
strength.
— Velleius Paterculus, Historiae Romanae

326.

Credo ut intelligam.
I believe in order to understand.
— Augustine, Sermons

327.

Cuiusque morum custos est quisque.
Each person is the guardian of their own conduct.
— Latin proverb

328.

Ars longa, vita brevis.
Art is long, life is short.
— Hippocrates (Greek maxim in Latin form)

329.

Cicero pro domo sua.
Cicero in defense of his own house.
— Cicero, Pro domo sua

This phrase comes from a speech Cicero delivered in 57 BC to reclaim his house on the Palatine Hill, which had been confiscated and dedicated to a temple by his political enemies. More broadly, the expression has come to mean defending one's own rights, interests, or property against injustice. Today it can be used figuratively when someone argues passionately for their own cause, often with a tone of self-interest or personal stake.

330.

Facile est principiis obsta.
It is easy to resist things at their beginnings.
— Caesar, De Bello Gallico

331.

Ars docendi.
The art of teaching.
— Latin proverb

332.

Concordia civium murus urbium.
The harmony of citizens is the wall of cities.
— Latin proverb

333.

Crescit amor nummi, quantum ipsa pecunia crescit.
The love of money grows as money itself grows.
— Juvenal, Satires

334.

Ars artis gratia.
Art for art's sake.
— Modern Latin motto

335.

Nemo mortalium omnibus horis sapit.
No mortal is wise at all times.
— Aulus Gellius, Noctes Atticae

336.

Certa amittimus, dum incerta petimus.
We lose the certain while we seek the uncertain.
— Pliny the Younger, Epistulae

337.

Non quia difficilia sunt non audemus, sed quia non audemus difficilia sunt.
It is not because things are difficult that we do not dare, but because we do not dare that they are difficult.
— Seneca, Epistulae morales

338.

Beati pauperes spiritu.
Blessed are the poor in spirit.
— Vulgate, Gospel of Matthew

339.

Citius, altius, fortius.
Faster, higher, stronger.
— Olympic motto in Latin

340.

Curiositas inimica est veritatis.
Curiosity is the enemy of truth.
— Augustine, Confessiones

341.

Facilius est Herculi clavam auferre quam rhetori verbum.
It is easier to take the club from Hercules than a word from a rhetorician.
— Jerome, Epistulae

342.

Credo quia absurdum.
I believe because it is absurd.
— Tertullian, De carne Christi

343.

Cibus, vinum, somnus, Venus omnia moderata bona.
Food, wine, sleep, love: all good things, if in moderation.
— Latin proverb

344.

Circulus vitiosus.
Vicious circle.
— Latin philosophical expression

345.

Ceteris paribus.
Other things being equal.
— Latin expression

346.

Nemo plus iuris transferre potest quam ipse habet.
No one can transfer more right than he himself has.
— Digest, Ulpian

347.

Semper Fidelis.
Always Faithful.
— Motto of the US Marine Corps (USMC)

348.

Ave Caesar, morituri te salutant.
Hail, Caesar, those who are about to die salute you.
— Suetonius, De vita Caesarum

349.

De Oppresso Liber.
To Free the Oppressed.
— Motto of the US Army Special Forces (Green Berets)

350.

Divide et impera.
Divide and rule.
— Roman political maxim

This strategy rests on a simple idea: weaken a potentially hostile group by splitting it into rival factions, making it easier to control. Attributed to Philip II of Macedon and later used extensively by the Romans, it became a staple of imperial policy and political handbooks. Today the phrase is often invoked with a critical tone, describing leaders or systems that maintain power by fostering division. It can also be applied more broadly to competition and rivalries that prevent unity.

351.

Dum Romae consulitur, Saguntum expugnatur.
While Rome debates, Saguntum is taken.
— Livy, Ab urbe condita

352.

Dies diem docet.
One day teaches another.
— Aulus Gellius, Noctes Atticae

353.

Excusatio non petita, accusatio manifesta.
An excuse not asked for is an obvious accusation.
— Latin proverb of legal and rhetorical tradition

354.

Veritas vos liberabit.
The truth will set you free.
— Vulgate, Gospel of John

355.

Felix qui nihil debet.
Happy is he who owes nothing.
— Latin proverb

356.

Fugit irreparabile tempus.
Time flies irretrievably.
— Virgil, Georgics

357.

Dum inter homines sumus, colamus humanitatem.
As long as we are among human beings, let us cultivate humanity.
— Seneca, Epistulae morales

358.

Saepe creat molles aspera spina rosas.
A harsh thorn often produces delicate roses.
— Ovid, Ars amatoria

359.

Nolite iudicare, ut non iudicemini.
Judge not, that you be not judged.
— Vulgate, Gospel of Matthew

360.

Nullum magnum ingenium sine mixtura dementiae fuit.
There has never been a great genius without a touch of madness.
— Seneca, De tranquillitate animi

361.

Alter ego
Another self, a second identity or trusted person.
— Common Latin expression

362.

Ubi caritas et amor, Deus ibi est.
Where charity and love are, there is God.
— Latin liturgical hymn

363.

Consensus facit nuptias
Consent makes marriage.
— Roman legal maxim

In Roman law, marriage did not arise from a religious rite but from the free and mutual will of the spouses. This revolutionary idea placed the individual above family and community obligations. The principle strongly influenced European matrimonial law and still underlies many aspects of modern legislation on marriage.

364.

Vice versa
The other way around, conversely.
— Common Latin expression

365.

Et cetera
And so on, and the rest.
— Common Latin expression

366.

Patres nostri magnae virtutis fuerunt.
Our fathers were of great virtue.
— Cato the Elder (Cato the Censor)

367.

Sunt lacrimae rerum et mentem mortalia tangunt.
There are tears for human things, and mortality touches the heart.
— Virgil, Aeneis

368.

Salus populi suprema lex esto.
The welfare of the people shall be the supreme law.
— Cicero, De legibus

369.

Quo usque tandem abutere, Catilina, patientia nostra?
How long, Catiline, will you abuse our patience?
— Cicero, In Catilinam

370.

Mens sana in corpore sano.
A sound mind in a sound body.
— Juvenal, Satires

371.

Corrupti mores, pravae leges.
When morals are corrupt, laws are perverted.
— Tacitus, Annals

372.

Nihil est miserum nisi cum putes.
Nothing is miserable unless you think it so.
— Boethius, Consolatio Philosophiae

373.

Fructus temporum.
The fruit of the times.
— Latin proverb

374.

Crimina morte extinguuntur.
Crimes are extinguished by death.
— Roman criminal law maxim

375.

Omnia mutantur, nihil interit.
Everything changes, nothing perishes.
— Ovid, Metamorphoses

376.

Consuetudine homines fere ad imperia parendum parati sunt.
By habit men are almost always ready to obey commands.
— Caesar, De Bello Civili

377.

Si Deus pro nobis, quis contra nos?
If God is for us, who can be against us?
— Vulgate, Epistle to the Romans

378.

Ne bis in idem.
Not twice for the same thing.
— Roman legal maxim

379.

Panem et circenses.
Bread and circuses.
— Juvenal, Satires

Juvenal coined this phrase in a satirical attack on the Roman people, who, he argued, had abandoned civic life and political responsibility in exchange for free food and public entertainment. Over time, it became a proverbial way of criticizing rulers who pacify or control the masses by offering material goods and distractions instead of freedom and participation.

380.

Radix omnium malorum est cupiditas.
La radice di tutti i mali è la cupidigia.
— Vulgata, Epistula I ad Timotheum

381.

Humilitas est mater virtutum.
Humility is the mother of virtues.
— Gregory the Great, Moralia in Iob

382.

Divina eloquia cum legente crescunt.
The divine words grow with the one who reads them.
— Gregory the Great, Homilies on Ezekiel

383.

Cornix cornici nunquam oculos effodit.
One crow never plucks out another crow's eyes.
— Latin proverb

384.

Ignorantia legis non excusat.
Ignorance of the law excuses no one.
— Roman legal maxim

385.

Cantabit vacuus coram latrone viator.
The traveler with nothing will sing before the robber.
— Juvenal, Satires

386.

Id est (i.e.)
That is, in other words.
— Common Latin expression

387.

Aurora aurum in ore habet.
The dawn has gold in its mouth.
— Latin proverb

388.

Amor tussisque non celatur.
Love and a cough cannot be concealed.
— Latin proverb

389.

Naturam expelles furca, tamen usque recurret.
You may drive out nature with a pitchfork, but she will always return.
— Horace, Epistles

390.

Veni, vidi, vici.
I came, I saw, I conquered.
— Julius Caesar

This famous phrase was used by Julius Caesar in a message to the Roman Senate to announce his swift victory over Pharnaces, king of Pontus, at the Battle of Zela in 47 BC. In just three words, Caesar captured speed, decisiveness, and efficiency, turning a military report into a timeless motto. Today the expression is quoted whenever someone wants to celebrate a quick and decisive success, conveying the energy of overcoming a challenge without hesitation.

391.

Homo sum: humani nihil a me alienum puto.
I am human, and nothing human is foreign to me.
— Terence, Heautontimorumenos

392.

Stultum est timere quod vitari non potest.
It is foolish to fear what cannot be avoided.
— Publilius Syrus, Sententiae

393.

Amicitia semper prodest, amor etiam aliquando nocet.
Friendship always benefits, love sometimes even harms.
— Pliny the Younger, Epistulae

394.

Pater noster, qui es in caelis.
Our Father, who art in heaven.
— The Lord's Prayer, recited in the Mass

395.

Qui tacet consentire videtur.
He who is silent is taken to consent.
— Medieval legal maxim

396.

Virtus post nummos.
Virtue after money.
— Juvenal, Satires

397.

Nullum magnum exemplum sine aliquo malo est.
No great example is without some flaw.
— Velleius Paterculus, Historiae Romanae

398.

Omnes homines natura aequales sunt.
All human beings are equal by nature.
— Ulpian, Digesta

399.

Forsan et haec olim meminisse iuvabit.
Perhaps someday it will be a joy to remember even these things.
— Virgil, Aeneid

400.

Qui multos vult esse discipulos, nullus est magister.
He who wants to have too many disciples is a teacher to none.
— Jerome, Epistulae

Jerome wrote this in a letter of advice to the young priest Nepotian, stressing the importance of sincerity and focus in teaching. The idea is that a true teacher should not seek popularity or collect disciples indiscriminately, but rather dedicate himself to guiding a smaller number with care and integrity. Over time, the phrase has been quoted to warn against ambition in leadership, superficial influence, or the temptation to please everyone instead of providing genuine instruction.

6

Amor Fati (401 – 500)

401.

Felix qui nihil debet.
Happy is he who owes nothing.
— Latin proverb

402.

Amicitia pares aut accipit aut facit.
Friendship either finds equals or makes them.
— Petronius, Satyricon

403.

Nolite iudicare, ut non iudicemini.
Judge not, that you be not judged.
— Vulgate, Gospel of Matthew

404.

Amori finem tempus, non animus facit.
It is time that ends love, not the will.
— Publilius Syrus, Sententiae

405.

Esto perpetua.
Let it be perpetual.
— Motto of Idaho

406.

Casus belli.
Cause of war.
— Latin expression

Literally *"cause of war,"* this Latin expression refers to the formal, real, or alleged reason a state gives to justify going to war. In history, a casus belli could be a concrete event (such as an attack or a diplomatic insult) or a pretext created to legitimize a conflict that was already decided. Today, it is often used figuratively to mean any excuse or pretext for a clash — political, legal, or even personal — beyond the military context.

407.

Vox in deserto.
A voice in the desert.
— Vulgate, Isaiah

408.

Generosa vis amoris.
The force of love is generous.
— Latin proverb

409.

Sapientia est potentia.
Wisdom is power.
— Latin proverb

410.

Cuius regio, eius religio.
Whose realm, his religion.
— Legal formula, Peace of Augsburg

411.

Salus aegroti suprema lex.
The health of the patient is the supreme law.
— Latin motto

412.

Fortuna labilis.
Fortune is fickle.
— Latin proverb

413.

Post tenebras lux.
After darkness, light.
— Renaissance Latin motto

414.

Homo animal rationale mortale.
Man is a rational and mortal animal.
— Isidore of Seville, Etymologiae

415.

Virtus difficilia amat.
Virtue loves difficult things.
— Seneca, Epistulae morales

416.

Pacta conventa.
Agreements stipulated.
— Latin legal maxim

417.

Agnus Dei, qui tollis peccata mundi, miserere nobis.
Lamb of God, you take away the sins of the world, have mercy on us.
— Catholic liturgy, Mass

418.

Pro bono
For the public good; professional work done free of charge.
— Latin legal expression

419.

Amor fati.
Love of fate.
— Stoic tradition

This Stoic expression means *"love of fate."* It is not just about accepting what happens in life, but embracing it fully — including suffering, loss, and hardship — as necessary parts of existence. To love one's fate is to see every event, pleasant or painful, as meaningful and essential, rather than wishing it were otherwise. Today, " *amor fati"* is often used as a reminder to practice resilience and gratitude, turning even difficulties into opportunities for growth.

420.

Non plus ultra.
No further beyond.
— Latin motto (attributed to the Pillars of Hercules)

421.

Ad hoc.
Made for this purpose, for this specific case.
— Latin expression

422.

Praemonitus, praemunitus.
Forewarned is forearmed.
— Latin proverb

423.

Plurima fames causa est .
Hunger is the cause of many evils.
— Seneca, Epistulae morales

424.

Requiescat in pace.
Rest in peace.
— Latin liturgical formula

425.

Veritas simplex oratio est.
Truth's speech is simple.
— Seneca, Epistulae morales

426.

Annus mirabilis.
Wonderful year.
— Classical Latin expression

427.

SPQR – Senatus Populusque Romanus.
The Senate and the Roman People.
— Official inscription of ancient Rome

428.

Fama volat.
Rumor flies.
— Virgil, Aeneid

429.

Non est vivere sed valere vita est.
Life is not just living, but living well.
— Martial, Epigrams

430.

Stultorum infinitus est numerus.
The number of fools is infinite.
— Vulgate, Ecclesiastes

431.

Ignis aurum probat, miseria fortes viros.
Fire tests gold, adversity tests strong men.
— Seneca, De providentia

432.

Non omnis qui habent citharam sunt citharoedi.
Not everyone who owns a lyre is a lyre player.
— Varro, De lingua Latina

433.

Lupus est agnis quicquid agit.
Whatever he does, he is a wolf to the lambs.
— Plautus, Asinaria

434.

Nulla est enim maior voluptas quam discendi cupiditas.
There is no greater pleasure than the desire to learn.
— Pliny the Younger, Epistulae

435.

Amicitia inter bonos contracta facile dirumpitur.
Friendship contracted among good men is not easily broken.
— Aulus Gellius, Noctes Atticae

436.

Nihil est quod magis decet principem quam aequitas.
Nothing befits a ruler more than fairness.
— Cassiodorus, Variae

437.

Praedicatio valet plus vita quam sermone.
Preaching is worth more by life than by words.
— Gregory the Great, Homiliae in Evangelia

438.

Tam mala sunt vicina quam proxima.
Neighbors are as troublesome as close relatives.
— Martial, Epigrammata

439.

Qualis rex, talis grex.
Like king, like people.
— Latin proverb

440.

Amor verus numquam moritur.
True love never dies.
— Latin proverb

441.

Initium sapientiae timor Domini.
The beginning of wisdom is the fear of the Lord.
— Vulgate, Proverbs

442.

Satius est aliena insania frui quam sua.
It is better to enjoy another's folly than your own.
— Seneca, Epistulae morales

443.

Amor magister optimus.
Love is the best teacher.
— Latin proverb

444.

Suum cuique tribuere.
To give each his due.
— Ulpian, Digesta

This maxim is part of the Roman law triad that summed up its fundamental principles: *honeste vivere* (to live honestly), *alterum non laedere* (to harm no one), and *suum cuique tribuere* (to give each his due). It goes beyond property or material goods: it is about recognizing for every person what belongs to them by right and dignity. Today, the phrase is still powerful. It is cited to call for fairness, respect for merit and responsibility, and as a moral reminder to treat all people with justice.

445.

Omnia tempus edax depascitur.
Time, the devourer, consumes all things.
— Seneca, Epistulae morales

446.

Tantum religio potuit suadere malorum.
So great the evils religion could persuade.
— Lucretius, De rerum natura

447.

Si vis beatus esse, ama virtutem: sola virtus beatum facit.
If you wish to be happy, love virtue: only virtue makes one happy.
— Boethius, Consolatio Philosophiae

448.

Volenti non fit iniuria.
No wrong is done to one who consents.
— Ulpian, Digesta

449.

Omnia fortuita in malis ducenda sunt.
All accidents must be counted among evils.
— Boethius, Consolatio Philosophiae

450.

Virtus sola nobilitat.
Only virtue makes one noble.
— Latin proverb

451.

Caritas omnia suffert.
Charity endures all things.
— Vulgate, Prima Epistula ad Corinthios

452.

Contra principia negantem non est disputandum.
There is no disputing with one who denies principles.
— Aristotle, Latin formula

453.

Lux mea lex.
My light is my law.
— Medieval Latin motto

454.

Donec eris felix, multos numerabis amicos.
As long as you are fortunate, you will count many friends.
— Ovid, Tristia

455.

Omne initium difficile est.
Every beginning is difficult.
— Latin proverb

456.

Fata viam invenient.
The fates will find a way.
— Virgil, Aeneis

457.

Vanitas vanitatum et omnia vanitas.
Vanity of vanities, all is vanity.
— Vulgate, Ecclesiastes

458.

In cauda venenum.
The poison is in the tail.
— Latin proverb

this proverb comes from the image of a scorpion, harmless at first glance but dangerous at the end. It warns that the most harmful part of something may come last. In literature and rhetoric, it refers to a speech, text, or action that hides its sting until the conclusion. In modern usage, it often describes situations where the danger, insult, or problem is revealed only at the end — like the fine print of a contract or a sudden twist in a negotiation.

459.

Aliquando et insanire iucundum est.
Sometimes it is pleasant even to be mad.
— Seneca, De tranquillitate animi

460.

Omnia mea mecum porto.
All that is mine I carry with me.
— Bias of Priene, Latin tradition

461.

Misericordia Dei super omnia.
The mercy of God is above all things.
— Latin religious proverb

462.

Dominus illuminatio mea.
The Lord is my light.
— Vulgate, Psalmi

463.

Noli me tangere.
Do not touch me.
— Vulgate, Gospel of John

464.

Res inter alios acta.
A thing agreed between others can neither harm nor benefit third parties.
— Roman civil law maxim

465.

Otiosi otium habent negotiosum.
The idle have a busy idleness.
— Suetonius, Vita Divi Augusti

466.

Clausula rebus sic stantibus
Clause valid as long as circumstances remain unchanged.
— Latin legal expression

467.

Deus ex machina.
God from the machine.
— Latin theatrical expression, from Euripides

This expression comes from ancient theater, where a mechanical device
(the *machina*) lowered an actor playing a god onto the stage to resolve
a seemingly unsolvable plot. In classical drama, it was a way to bring
about a sudden, divine resolution. In modern usage, it refers to any
unexpected, improbable intervention that abruptly solves a problem
in a story — often criticized as artificial or unconvincing.

468.

Pueri pueri, puerilia tractant.
Children are children and busy themselves with childish things.
— Latin proverb

469.

Ars docendi.
The art of teaching.
— Latin proverb

470.

Summum ius, summa iniuria.
The strictest law is the greatest injustice.
— Cicero, De officiis

471.

Nihil est enim tam angusti animi quam amare .
Nothing is more narrow-minded than to love riches.
— Cicero, De officiis

472.

Sunt aliquid Manes; letum non omnia finit.
The spirits of the dead are something; death does not end all.
— Propertius, Elegiae

473.

Dum vivimus, vivamus.
While we live, let us live.
— Publilius Syrus, Sententiae

474.

Mutatis mutandis.
The necessary changes having been made.
— Latin expression

475.

Spes animos levat adversis oppressos.
Hope lifts spirits pressed down by adversity.
— Prudentius, Psychomachia

476.

Omnia orta occidunt et aucta senescunt.
All things that arise perish, and what grows old decays.
— Sallust, Bellum Catilinae

477.

Nulla dies sine linea.
No day without a line.
— Pliny the Elder, Naturalis Historia

478.

Gallina scripsit.
The hen has written.
— Latin humorous proverb

This Latin saying was used to joke about sloppy or illegible handwriting, much like the modern phrase "chicken scratch." The image comes from the marks left by styluses on wax tablets or ink on parchment, resembling the scratches of a hen's claws. Today, it can still be used in a humorous way, drawing a playful connection between the classrooms of antiquity and those of today: some flaws — like bad handwriting — never seem to change.

479.

Salus populi suprema lex esto.
Let the welfare of the people be the supreme law.
— Cicero, De legibus

480.

Auri sacra fames.
Accursed hunger for gold.
— Virgil, Aeneis

481.

Veritas numquam perit.
Truth never perishes.
— Seneca, Epistulae morales

482.

Ubi emendari non potest, delendum est.
What cannot be corrected must be erased.
— Quintilian, Institutio Oratoria

483.

Carthago delenda est.
Carthage must be destroyed.
— Cato the Censor

484.

Virtus repulsae nescia sordidae.
Virtue knows nothing of shameful defeat.
— Silius Italicus, Punica

485.

Fiat lux.
Let there be light.
— Vulgate, Genesis

This formula opens the biblical account of Creation in Genesis (1:3), preserved in the Latin Vulgate translation by Saint Jerome. In just two words, it evokes the moment when the world emerged from darkness. Over time, it has become a universal motto for new beginnings, for the arrival of clarity after obscurity, or for the flash of discovery that dispels ignorance. Today it is quoted in religious, literary, ironic, and everyday contexts — whenever one wishes to highlight the sudden appearance of light or an idea.

486.

Annuit coeptis.
He [God] has favored our undertakings.
— Motto on the Great Seal of the United States

487.

Quid est aliud miserum esse quam tempus male uti?
What is being unhappy, if not using time badly?
— Seneca, De brevitate vitae

488.

Aliquando bonus dormitat Homerus.
Sometimes even good Homer nods.
— Horace, Ars poetica

489.

O curas hominum! O quantum est in rebus inane!
O the cares of men! O how much emptiness there is in things!
— Persius, Saturae

490.

Nihil est quod non vincat amor.
There is nothing that love does not conquer.
— Claudian, De bello Gildonico

491.

Dilige et quod vis fac.
Love, and do what you will.
— Augustine, In epistulam Ioannis

492.

Nulla fides regni sociis.
There is no loyalty among partners in power.
— Lucan, Pharsalia

493.

Contentus parvo securus ab omni turbine.
Content with little, safe from every storm.
— Tibullus, Elegiae

494.

Magnitudo animi in tolerando est.
Greatness of soul lies in enduring.
— Seneca, De vita beata

This maxim from Seneca means "Greatness of soul lies in enduring." It reflects a central Stoic idea: true strength is not found in conquest or domination, but in the ability to bear hardships with dignity and patience. In ancient philosophy, it was a call to resilience — facing pain, loss, or injustice without being broken. Today, it is often quoted as a reminder that endurance and inner composure are marks of real character, more than power or success.

495.

Dilige amicos, sed veritatem magis.
Love your friends, but love truth more.
— Aristotle, Latin tradition

496.

Pax optima rerum.
Peace is the best of things.
— Silius Italicus, Punica

497.

Concordia magnae res crescunt.
By concord great things grow.
— Sallust, Bellum Iugurthinum

498.

Contra vim mortis non est medicamen in hortis.
Against the power of death there is no remedy in the gardens.
— Latin proverb

499.

In lumine tuo videbimus lumen.
In your light we shall see light.
— Motto of Columbia University

500.

Abusus non tollit usum.
Abuse does not take away proper use.
— Latin maxim

7

Dulcis in Fundo (501 – 600)

501.

Nullum est iam dictum quod non dictum sit prius.
Nothing has been said that has not been said before.
— Terence, Eunuchus

502.

Ars poetica est non omnia dicere.
The art of poetry is not to say everything.
— Ovid, Ars amatoria

503.

Causarum ignoratio poenarum est mater.
Ignorance of causes is the mother of suffering.
— Cicero, De natura deorum

504.

Celeritas in periculis virtus est.
Swiftness in danger is a virtue.
— Sallust, Bellum Catilinae

505.

Romanus sum.
I am a Roman citizen.
— Cicero, In Verrem

In ancient Rome, these two words carried enormous weight. To say *Romanus sum* was to claim the full protection, rights, and privileges of Roman citizenship anywhere in the empire. Cicero used this phrase in his prosecution against the corrupt governor Verres, to highlight the outrage of abusing a Roman citizen in Sicily. For Romans, citizenship was more than legal status — it was identity, dignity, and power. Today, the phrase can be understood as a proud declaration of belonging to a community that guarantees justice and rights.

506.

Concordia parvae res crescunt, discordia maximae dilabuntur.
With harmony, small things grow; with discord, even the greatest collapse.
— Sallust, Bellum Iugurthinum

507.

Consuetudo est optima legum interpres.
Custom is the best interpreter of laws.
— Cicero, Pro Cluentio

508.

Non sum ego qui fueram.
I am no longer the man I once was.
— Propertius, Elegiae

509.

Nihil est turpius quam gloriam quaerere ex calamitate alterius.
Nothing is more disgraceful than seeking glory from another's misfortune.
— Aulus Gellius, Noctes Atticae

510.

Nil est ab omni parte beatum.
Nothing is blessed in every respect.
— Claudian, De Raptu Proserpinae

511.

Pueri ad voluptatem celerius quam ad laborem incitantur.
Children are moved more quickly by pleasure than by effort.
— Quintilian, Institutio Oratoria

512.

Dies irae, dies illa.
Day of wrath, that day.
— Medieval hymn

513.

De gustibus non est disputandum.
There is no disputing about tastes.
— Latin proverb

This is one of the most famous Latin proverbs, and it's still widely quoted today. The Romans used it to remind people that personal preferences — whether in food, art, or love — are subjective and not open to rational debate. What delights one person may leave another indifferent, and neither is "wrong." Over the centuries, the phrase has survived almost unchanged in many modern languages, a sign of its timeless resonance. In English, it is often paraphrased as *"There's no accounting for taste."*

514.

Fiunt, non nascuntur Christiani.
Christians are made, not born.
— Tertullian, Apologeticum

515.

Dulcis in fundo.
The sweet comes at the end.
— Latin proverb

516.

Errare humanum est.
To err is human.
— Seneca, Epistulae morales

517.

Et tu, Brute?
And you, Brutus?
— Suetonius, Divus Iulius

518.

Ecce homo.
Behold the man.
— Vulgate, Gospel of John

According to the Gospel of John (19:5), these are the words spoken by Pontius Pilate as he presented the scourged Jesus to the crowd before the crucifixion. In Christian tradition, *Ecce homo* symbolizes both suffering and dignity. In modern usage, the phrase can also be applied more broadly when pointing out someone exposed to judgment or vulnerability.

519.

Exegi monumentum aere perennius.
I have raised a monument more lasting than bronze.
— Horace, Odes

520.

Omne ignotum pro magnifico est.
Everything unknown is taken as grand.
— Tacitus, Agricola

521.

Exitus acta probat.
The outcome justifies the deeds.
— Ovid, Heroides

522.

Ob torto collo.
With the neck twisted (under compulsion).
— Latin expression

523.

Festina lente.
Make haste slowly.
— Suetonius, Life of Augustus

524.

Ubi societas, ibi ius.
Where there is society, there is law.
— Roman legal maxim

525.

Fortis cadere, cedere non potest.
The strong may fall, but cannot yield.
— Latin proverb

526.

Frangit inertia vires.
Inertia breaks strength.
— Ovid, Metamorphoses

527.

Fronti nulla fides.
No trust should be placed in appearances.
— Ovid, Ars amatoria

528.

Gens una sumus.
We are one people.
— Latin motto

529.

Gloria in excelsis Deo.
Glory to God in the highest.
— Liturgical hymn

530.

Graecia capta ferum victorem cepit.
Greece, once conquered, conquered its fierce victor.
— Horace, Epistulae

531.

Hannibal ad portas.
Hannibal is at the gates.
— Livy, Ab urbe condita

532.

Manu militari.
By military force.
— Latin legal expression

533.

Homo homini sacra res.

Man is a sacred thing to man.
— Seneca, Epistulae morales

534.

Hostis honesta est.

An honorable enemy is a kind of honor.
— Latin proverb

535.

Ibi victoria, ubi concordia.

Where there is unity, there is victory.
— Latin proverb

536.

Ignorantia iuris nocet.

Ignorance of the law harms.
— Roman legal maxim

537.

Imperare sibi maximum imperium est.

To rule oneself is the greatest power.
— Seneca, Epistulae morales

538.

Ubi pater, ibi patria.

Where the father is, there is the homeland.
— Latin proverb

539.

In dubio libertas.

In doubt, liberty.
— Legal motto

540.

In hoc signo vinces.

In this sign you will conquer.
— Eusebius of Caesarea, Vita Constantini

541.

In medio stat virtus.

Virtue stands in the middle.
— Latin proverb

This famous Latin saying expresses the idea that wisdom and moral integrity are found in balance, away from extremes. The concept originates in Greek philosophy, especially Aristotle's *Nicomachean Ethics*, where virtue is described as the "mean" (*mesotes*) between two vices: courage, for example, lies between recklessness and cowardice. In Latin, the closest phrasing appears in Horace's Epistles (I, 18, 9): *Virtus est medium vitiorum et utrimque reductum* ("Virtue is the mean between vices, distant from either extreme"). Today, it is often cited as a reminder that true strength and stability come not from extremes, but from moderation and balance.

542.

Absit iniuria verbis.

Let there be no offense in words.
— Livy, Ab Urbe Condita

543.

Satis superque meo de sanguine luctus.
Too much, and more than enough, of sorrow from my blood.
— Tibullus, Elegiae

544.

Actori incumbit probatio.
The burden of proof rests on the accuser.
— Roman legal maxim

545.

Ipse dixit.
He himself said it.
— Pythagorean tradition in Latin

The phrase *ipse dixit* originally referred to the authority of Pythagoras, the ancient Greek philosopher. His followers would settle debates simply by saying, "He himself said it," as if the master's word required no further proof. In time, the expression became a way to describe any claim accepted without evidence, purely on authority. Today, it survives in English as *"ipse dixit"* to criticize arguments based only on assertion: when someone expects you to believe something just because they said so, without offering reasons or proof.

546.

Ira furor brevis est.
Anger is a brief madness.
— Horace, Epistulae

547.

Ite missa est.
Go, the Mass is ended.
— Catholic liturgy

548.

Lacrimae rerum sunt.
They are the tears of things.
— Virgil, Aeneid

549.

Laudator temporis acti.
A praiser of times past.
— Horace, Ars poetica

550.

Agnus Dei, qui tollis peccata mundi, miserere nobis.
Lamb of God, you take away the sins of the world, have mercy on us.
— Ordinary of the Mass

551.

Lex posterior derogat priori.
A later law repeals an earlier one.
— Roman legal maxim

552.

Libertas perfundet omnia luce.
Liberty will flood everything with light.
— Latin hymn

553.

Alii clari factis, alii scriptis fiunt.
Some become famous through deeds, others through writings.
— Sallust, Bellum Catilinae

554.

Lupus in fabula.
The wolf in the story.
— Terence, Adelphoe

This saying appears in Terence's comedy *Adelphoe* and corresponds to the modern English saying "speak of the devil." In ancient Rome, people believed that mentioning the wolf could make it appear, so the sudden arrival of someone being talked about was linked to the feared animal. The expression has survived into modern languages with the same playful meaning: you say it when a person shows up right while they were being discussed, as if conjured by the conversation.

555.

Macte animo!
Take courage!
— Virgil, Aeneid

556.

Magna est veritas et praevalebit.
Great is the truth, and it will prevail.
— Vulgate, Ezra

557.

Magnum vectigal est parsimonia.
Thrift is a great revenue.
— Cicero, Philippicae

558.

Male parta, male dilabuntur.
What is wrongfully gained is wrongfully lost.
— Cicero, Philippicae

559.

Manus manum lavat.
One hand washes the other.
— Petronius, Satyricon

560.

Mater artium necessitas.
Necessity is the mother of the arts.
— Latin proverb

561.

Mater dolorosa.
Sorrowful Mother.
— Liturgical title

562.

Medice, cura te ipsum.
Physician, heal thyself.
— Vulgate, Gospel of Luke

563.

Dulce et decorum est pro patria mori.
It is sweet and fitting to die for one's country.
— Horace, Odes

564.

Mihi cura futuri.
My concern is for the future.
— Latin motto

565.

Miserere mei, Domine.
Have mercy on me, Lord.
— Vulgate, Psalms

566.

Mors omnia solvit.
Death dissolves everything.
— Seneca, Epistulae morales

567.

Mater semper certa est, pater numquam.
La madre è sempre certa, il padre mai.
— Roman legal maxim

568.

Malum est consilium quod mutari non potest.
Bad is the plan that cannot be changed.
— Publilius Syrus, Sententiae

569.

Vita rustica melius paratur quam urbana.
Country life is better ordered than city life.
— Columella, De Re Rustica

570.

Ne bis in idem.
Not twice for the same thing.
— Legal maxim

571.

Ne quid nimis.
Nothing in excess.
— Terence, Andria

572.

Nemo potest personam diu ferre fictam.
No one can wear a false mask for long.
— Seneca, De clementia

573.

Nemo sine vitio est.
No one is without fault.
— Seneca, De vita beata

574.

Nil difficile volenti.
Nothing is difficult for the willing.
— Latin proverb

575.

Paupertas pati consuetudo est optima.

The best preparation for poverty is getting used to it.
— Publilius Syrus, Sententiae

576.

Non omnis moriar.

I shall not wholly die.
— Horace, Odes

577.

Legum servi sumus ut liberi esse possimus.

We are servants of the laws so that we may be free.
— Cassiodorus, Variae

578.

Non sibi, sed patriae.

Not for self, but for country.
— Latin motto

579.

Nosce te ipsum.

Know yourself.
— Delphic maxim (Latin tradition)

580.

Scis etenim iustum gemina suspendere lance anceps.

For you know it is just to weigh on a double scale with equal balance.
— Persius, Satires

581.

Numquam desperandum.
Never despair.
— Latin proverb

582.

Oblivionis nihil est nisi memoriae interitus.
Oblivion is nothing but the destruction of memory.
— Augustine, Confessiones

583.

Oderint dum metuant.
Let them hate, so long as they fear.
— Accius, Atreus

584.

Odi et amo.
I hate and I love.
— Catullus, Carmina

"I hate and I love" — so begins one of the most famous couplets of Catullus (*Carmina* 85). In just two words, the poet captures the contradiction of love, capable of bringing joy and torment at the same time. The full text reads: "*Odi et amo. Quare id faciam, fortasse requiris. Nescio, sed fieri sentio et excrucior.*" Translation: "I hate and I love. Perhaps you ask why I do so. I do not know, but I feel it happening and I am tormented." Catullus describes his bond with Lesbia, marked by passion and suffering, but the couplet became universal: an eternal synthesis of the ambivalence of human feelings.

585.

Caro salutis est cardo.
The flesh is the hinge of salvation.
— Tertullian, De Resurrectione Carnis

586.

Omnia mutantur, nos et mutamur in illis.
All things change, and we change with them.
— Latin proverb

587.

Omnia praetereunt.
All things pass.
— Latin proverb

588.

Optimus magister bonus liber.
The best teacher is a good book.
— Latin proverb

589.

Ora et labora.
Pray and work.
— Benedictine rule

590.

Orbis non sufficit.
The world is not enough.
— Latin motto

591.

Inclinatio animi est, ubi nullum est consilium.
Inclination of the mind prevails where there is no counsel.
— Velleius Paterculus, Historiae Romanae

592.

Parva scintilla saepe magnam flamman excitat.
A small spark often sets off a great flame.
— Latin proverb

593.

Pax optima rerum.
Peace is the best of things.
— Silius Italicus, Punica

594.

Vita sine litteris mors est.
Life without learning is death.
— Seneca, Epistulae morales

595.

Persona non grata.
Unwelcome person.
— Latin diplomatic expression

596.

Plenus venter non studet libenter.
A full belly does not like to study.
— Latin proverb

597.

Pons asinorum.
Bridge of donkeys.
— Latin scholastic expression

598.

Possunt quia posse videntur.
They can because they think they can.
— Virgil, Aeneid

599.

Pro domo sua.
In defense of one's own cause.
— Cicero, Pro domo sua

600.

Primus inter pares.
First among equals.
— Tacitus, Annales

This expression describes someone who, while part of a group of equals, occupies a position of preeminence. In ancient Rome it was used to present the emperor as merely the first among senators, preserving the appearance of republican continuity. In reality, his power was immense, though veiled under a façade of equality. Today, "first among equals" is used to describe a leader who holds authority while formally remaining on the same level as others.

8

The Voices Behind the Aphorisms

This final section offers a closer look at the great minds whose words echo throughout the pages of this book. Latin aphorisms did not appear in a vacuum: they were coined by poets, philosophers, historians, and statesmen whose lives and works shaped Western culture.

Their voices belong to different centuries and contexts— from the Roman Republic to the early Christian era—yet they share a common ability to distill universal truths into a few unforgettable words. Understanding who they were helps us appreciate not only the brilliance of their phrases, but also the world in which those phrases were born.

What follows is not an exhaustive encyclopedia, but a gallery of portraits: concise sketches of the authors most frequently cited in this collection. Each one contributed in a unique way to the enduring legacy of Latin wisdom, a legacy that still speaks to us today.

Augustine (354–430 AD)

Bishop of Hippo, philosopher, and one of the most influential Christian thinkers of all time. Augustine lived during the decline of the Roman Empire, a period of cultural and political turbulence that shaped his thought. Born in North Africa, he studied rhetoric and philosophy before converting to Christianity at the age of thirty-two, an event that marked a turning point in his life.

His writings combine classical learning with deep spiritual insight, bridging the worlds of Greco-Roman philosophy and Christian theology. The *Confessions*, written as an autobiographical prayer, is both a personal story of conversion and a profound meditation on memory, time, and the human heart's restless search for God. In *The City of God*, Augustine responds to the fall of Rome, arguing that earthly kingdoms rise and fall, but the "City of God" endures forever. The *Enchiridion* and other shorter works distill his moral and theological reflections in concise, memorable form.

Many Latin aphorisms attributed to Augustine carry a timeless resonance: they reflect not only religious faith, but also a universal search for meaning, justice, and truth. His voice, at once philosophical and pastoral, continues to echo through Western thought, influencing theology, ethics, and even modern discussions of the self.

Cicero (106–43 BC)

Marcus Tullius Cicero was Rome's greatest orator and one of its most versatile thinkers. Born into a wealthy equestrian family, he rose to prominence in politics, law, and literature during the turbulent final decades of the Roman Republic. His career was marked by brilliance in the courtroom and in the Senate, where his speeches combined sharp logic with powerful rhetorical artistry.

Cicero's works are among the most extensive in Latin literature. In *De oratore*, he explores the art of persuasion and the moral responsibility of the speaker. The *Tusculan Disputations* examine themes such as death, virtue, and happiness, bringing Stoic and Academic philosophy into Roman intellectual life. In *De legibus* and *De re publica*, he reflects on law, justice, and the ideal state, shaping concepts that would influence Western political thought for centuries.

Many of the aphorisms attributed to Cicero condense his view that eloquence must serve virtue and that law exists for the common good. His phrases—at once practical and idealistic—are still quoted in courts, classrooms, and public debates. Though executed during the power struggles that ended the Republic, Cicero left behind a legacy as both defender of liberty and master of words.

Horace (65–8 BC)

Quintus Horatius Flaccus, known simply as Horace, was one of the greatest poets of the Augustan age. Born to a freedman in southern Italy, he received an excellent education in Rome and Athens before fighting in the civil wars. Afterward, he became part of the literary circle around Maecenas, patron of the arts, and found lasting security under the reign of Augustus.

Horace's poetry blends elegance, wit, and philosophical reflection. His *Odes* celebrate friendship, love, and the fleeting nature of life, often urging readers to "seize the day" (*carpe diem*). In the *Epistles* and the *Ars poetica*, he reflects on the art of poetry, moderation, and the balance between pleasure and virtue.

Many of his maxims—brief, polished, and memorable—have become universal expressions of human experience. From reflections on time and fate to humorous advice on daily living, Horace's verses capture both the joy and the brevity of life. His voice remains one of the clearest windows into the spirit of Rome's golden literary age.

Juvenal (late 1st – early 2nd century AD)

Decimus Iunius Iuvenalis, or Juvenal, was the master of Roman satire. Little is known of his life, but his biting verses paint a vivid picture of imperial Rome under Domitian and his successors. His *Satires* expose vice, hypocrisy, and corruption with sharp wit and moral indignation.

Juvenal coined phrases that have outlived his era. Expressions like *mens sana in corpore sano* ("a sound mind in a sound body") and *panem et circenses* ("bread and circuses") reveal his ability to crystallize social criticism in unforgettable words. His work ranges from humorous exaggeration to serious critique, but always with the aim of unmasking human folly.

Though he often wrote with bitterness, Juvenal's voice remains powerful and relevant. His aphorisms remind us that satire is not only entertainment but also a mirror held up to society, reflecting truths that still resonate today.

Lucretius (c. 99–55 BC)

Titus Lucretius Carus was a Roman poet and philosopher best known for his epic poem *De rerum natura* (*On the Nature of Things*). Written in six books of hexameter verse, the work presents and defends the teachings of

Epicurus, offering a vision of the universe governed by natural laws rather than divine intervention.

Lucretius explains atomism, the mortality of the soul, and the pursuit of tranquility through reason. Though deeply philosophical, his poetry combines scientific curiosity with vivid imagery, making abstract ideas memorable and compelling. His famous maxim *ex nihilo nihil fit* ("nothing comes from nothing") captures the rational spirit of his work.

Largely ignored in his own time, Lucretius was rediscovered during the Renaissance, profoundly influencing modern science and philosophy. His voice represents one of the boldest attempts in antiquity to reconcile poetry and reason, showing that beauty and truth can coexist in verse.

Martial (c. 40–104 AD)

Marcus Valerius Martialis, known as Martial, perfected the Latin epigram. Born in Spain, he moved to Rome, where he spent most of his life writing sharp, concise verses that captured the wit and vices of urban society.

His *Epigrams*—over 1,500 short poems—range from playful observations to biting satire. Many are just a few lines long, yet they distill entire situations or characters with precision. Martial often mocked pretension, vanity, and corruption, but he also celebrated friendship, leisure, and the pleasures of daily life.

From him come some of the shortest yet most enduring Latin sayings. His legacy lies in showing how brevity can strike harder than long speeches, turning wit into wisdom.

Ovid (43 BC – 17 AD)

Publius Ovidius Naso, or Ovid, was one of Rome's most inventive poets. Born in Sulmo, he rose quickly in literary circles with works full of elegance, wit, and emotional insight.

His masterpiece, the *Metamorphoses*, is a sweeping epic of myths and transformations that became a cornerstone of Western art and literature. In the *Ars amatoria* (*The Art of Love*) and the *Heroides*, he explored themes of desire, seduction, and the complexity of human relationships.

Exiled by Emperor Augustus to the remote town of Tomis on the Black Sea, Ovid continued to write until his death. His verses, rich in imagination and irony, left behind unforgettable aphorisms and stories that still resonate today.

Seneca (c. 4 BC – 65 AD)

Lucius Annaeus Seneca, known as Seneca the Younger, was a Stoic philosopher, statesman, and dramatist whose life reflected the tensions of Rome's early empire. Born in Corduba (modern Córdoba, Spain), he was educated in rhetoric and philosophy in Rome and rose to prominence as both a writer and political figure.

Seneca's career was marked by triumph and peril. He served as tutor and later advisor to the young Nero, guiding the emperor in his early reign. Yet as Nero grew more tyrannical, Seneca withdrew from court life, eventually accused of conspiracy and ordered to take his own life. His death, carried out with composure, became a final testament to his Stoic ideals.

His writings, however, are his true legacy. The *Letters to Lucilius* explore questions of virtue, mortality, and the wise use of time, offering philosophy in a deeply personal and practical form. Essays such as *On the Shortness of Life* and *On Providence* confront the brevity of existence and the unpredictability of fortune, urging resilience and inner freedom.

Seneca's aphorisms distill profound truths into concise, memorable lines, bridging abstract philosophy with daily experience. Both courtier and sage, he embodies the contradictions of his age, yet his voice continues to speak across centuries as a guide to self-mastery, courage, and clarity of mind.

Tacitus (c. 56 – c. 120 AD)

Publius Cornelius Tacitus was one of Rome's greatest historians, known for his sharp style and unflinching analysis of power. Serving as senator and consul, he witnessed the politics of the early empire firsthand.

His major works, the *Annals* and the *Histories*, recount the reigns of emperors from Tiberius to Domitian. Tacitus wrote with brevity and intensity, exposing corruption, tyranny, and the fragile balance between liberty and authority.

Many of his aphorisms—such as *corruptissima res publica plurimae leges* ("the more corrupt the state, the more numerous the laws")—reveal timeless political insights. His voice remains a model of historical honesty, blending moral judgment with literary brilliance.

Terence (c. 195–159 BC)

Publius Terentius Afer, known as Terence, was a North African-born playwright who became one of Rome's most refined dramatists. Six of his comedies survive, including *Andria* and *Heautontimorumenos*.

Admired for their elegant language and realistic characters, Terence's plays explore themes of family, love, and human weakness with subtle humor. His famous line *homo sum: humani nihil a me alienum puto* ("I am human: nothing human is foreign to me") reflects his deep empathy for human experience.

Terence's influence endured through the Renaissance, shaping European theater and moral thought.

Virgil (70–19 BC)

Publius Vergilius Maro, remembered simply as Virgil, was Rome's greatest poet and the author of its national epic. Born near Mantua in northern Italy, he studied philosophy, rhetoric, and Greek literature before becoming part of the literary circle of Maecenas, the close advisor of Augustus.

Virgil's literary career unfolded in three masterpieces. The *Eclogues* (*Bucolics*) are pastoral poems that blend rustic themes with subtle political allusions, presenting visions of harmony and renewal. The *Georgics* elevate the dignity of rural labor, transforming agriculture into a metaphor for resilience, order, and the bond between humanity and the natural world.

His crowning work, the *Aeneid*, tells the story of Aeneas, the Trojan hero whose journey to Italy symbolizes the divine mission of Rome. More than a tale of adventure, it weaves myth, history, and philosophy into a meditation on duty (*pietas*), sacrifice, and destiny. Left unfinished at his death in 19 BC, the poem nevertheless became the cornerstone of Roman cultural identity and an enduring model of epic poetry.

Virgil's verses—*arma virumque cano* ("I sing of arms and the man"), *omnia vincit amor* ("love conquers all")—are among the most quoted in Latin literature. Majestic yet humane, his poetry embodies the ideals and aspirations of Roman civilization, ensuring his place as one of the most influential voices in Western culture.

Appendix: Roman Numerals at a Glance

Roman numerals originated in ancient Rome and served for centuries as the official numbering system of the Roman Empire. Based on the use of Latin letters to represent numbers, this method was practical for recording dates, money, addresses, and especially for inscriptions and public records. Roman numerals were essential in administration, from counting legions and marking architectural projects to legal annotations and official decrees.

Even after the fall of the Western Roman Empire, the system survived throughout the Middle Ages. It was widely used in manuscripts and ecclesiastical documents, ensuring its preservation even as it was gradually replaced by the more versatile Arabic numeral system, better suited for complex calculations. Roman numerals never disappeared completely, maintaining a strong symbolic and decorative role.

Today they are still familiar: on clock faces, in the titles of monarchs and popes (Louis XIV, John Paul II), in book chapters, and on monuments. They are also used in cultural and sporting events, such as the Olympic Games and the Super Bowl—*Super Bowl LVII* for the 57th edition.

How the System Works

Roman numerals are built on seven main symbols:

- I = 1

- V = 5

- X = 10

- L = 50

- C = 100

- D = 500

- M = 1000

Addition: A smaller symbol after a larger one is added.

- VI = 5 + 1 = 6

- LX = 50 + 10 = 60

Subtraction: A smaller symbol before a larger one is subtracted.

- IV = 5 – 1 = 4

- IX = 10 – 1 = 9

- XC = 100 – 10 = 90

Repetition: A symbol may be repeated up to three times.

- III = 3

- XXX = 30

- CCC = 300

- MMM = 3000

Restrictions: Certain forms are avoided. For 400, "CD" is used instead of "CCCC"; for 900, "CM" instead of "DCCCC."

Fun Facts

- **No zero:** The system had no symbol for zero, one reason why it was eventually replaced by the Arabic numerals we use today.

- **Modern uses:** Roman numerals still appear in movie titles (*Rocky II*), in film credits, on memorials, and on both antique and modern clock faces.

- **Books and events:** Many books use Roman numerals for preliminary pages, and major events like the Olympic Games and the Super Bowl continue to use them to mark their editions.

- Though less practical for calculation, Roman numerals remain a living cultural legacy—symbols of tradition and continuity that still resonate across the Western world.

Dear Reader,
Thank you for choosing this book. Your support means a great deal to me.

If you enjoyed it, I would be truly grateful if you could leave a short review or simply a star rating on Amazon. This small gesture helps other readers discover the book and encourages my future projects.

Gratias ex animo!

Giulio Vitali